What Was the Tulsa Race Massacre of 1921?

by Caleb Gayle

illustrated by Tim Foley

Penguin Workshop

To peanut, to the fam, and to the kids who, like me,
didn't know the whole story—CG

For Craig & Vickie—TF

PENGUIN WORKSHOP
An imprint of Penguin Random House LLC, New York

First published in the United States of America by Penguin Workshop,
an imprint of Penguin Random House LLC, New York, 2023

Visit us online at penguinrandomhouse.com.

Library of Congress Control Number: 2022044822

Printed in the United States of America

ISBN 9780593521700 (paperback)   10 9 8 7 6 5 4 3 2   WOR
ISBN 9780593521717 (library binding)   10 9 8 7 6 5 4 3 2   WOR

Contents

What Was the Tulsa Race Massacre of 1921?

May 31, 1921

Tuesday was prom night for the students of Booker T. Washington High School in Tulsa, Oklahoma. Like other proms held in past years, kids would show up in suits and ties, dresses, and their best shoes. They would dance the foxtrot and the cakewalk to the popular music of the 1920s—jazz, ragtime, and barrelhouse.

Veneice Sims and Verby Ellison were going to the prom together. Veneice's parents were allowing her to stay out until midnight—a special treat. Veneice, much later in her life, remembered how she was looking forward to cutting loose on this fun night.

Usually, her dad would only let her play church music on the family's Victrola record player. At the prom, she planned to dance, dance, dance. Beforehand, she laid out her blue silk dress, silver shoes, and a pearl necklace borrowed for the night. She was living her best life. And why wouldn't she be?

Her dad was a mechanic for the bus company. She lived in a three-bedroom home in a nice neighborhood. She had enough money to have the kind of prom dress and shoes most girls dream of. Not to mention, the Sims family had a car.

By 1921, Veneice's parents had achieved the "American Dream" of success. This was especially remarkable because the Sims were Black. Not many other Black families (or white families) in America lived nearly as good a life as the Sims did. Even in the booming 1920s, nearly 60 percent of Americans were living in poverty, most of them Black people, immigrants, and farmers.

Named after the famous Black political leader, educator, and author, Booker T. Washington was an all-Black high school in the all-Black neighborhood where Veneice lived. It was called Greenwood, but to many it was better known as Black Wall Street.

Booker T. Washington

Black Wall Street covered thirty-five blocks. It got its nickname because of the many thriving businesses there. (Wall Street in New York City is a famous financial center.) Almost two hundred stores populated the area: hotels, restaurants, barbershops, two theaters, tailor shops, schools, a skating rink, and more. There was a public library, a hospital, a bus company, grocery stores, and about twelve churches. Many of the businesses were owned and operated by Black people. This was unusual back then. People who came

to visit were impressed. It seemed like this part
of the country—the southwestern United States,
where Oklahoma is—offered the best chance for

Black people to make a good life for themselves.

There were, however, dangers to living in a neighborhood like Greenwood.

All That Jazz

The essence of jazz is improvisation, redesigning and making up the structure and sound of a musical piece in real time. This includes a much more rhythmic and fluid way of presenting music. The roots of jazz can be found in the United States, primarily

in New Orleans, as Black musicians blended styles of swing, call-and-response, and bent and blue notes. It borrowed heavily from blues and ragtime. Today, jazz is played across the country. You can hear the influence of jazz in so many kinds of music, including R&B and hip-hop. It is the base from which many other musical stylings have emerged.

Black Wall Street and the white neighborhoods of Tulsa were separated. Some white people resented that this nearby Black community was doing so well. This made things very dangerous for Greenwood's Black people.

On prom night, before Veneice Sims got to slip into her beautiful blue dress, violence erupted in her neighborhood. White rioters began a brutal attack against the Black people in town. She heard men shouting, guns firing. All of a sudden, her dad was shouting to her, "There's a race riot. It's time to go."

Only twenty-four hours later, little of Black Wall Street was left standing. A massacre is when lots of innocent people are murdered, and their property destroyed. That's what happened in Greenwood. That's why this terrible event is known as the Tulsa Race Massacre of 1921. It was one of the worst instances of racial violence in US history.

CHAPTER 1
The Promise of Oklahoma

In the late nineteenth century, some parts of Tulsa, as well as other places now part of the state of Oklahoma, were becoming known as safe havens for Black families. Places where they could make new and better lives.

For decades, there had been Black people living in Oklahoma. They first came as enslaved people, but also as never-enslaved Black Native people of five tribal nations of Native Americans—the Chickasaw, Seminole, Cherokee, Choctaw, and Creek. These tribal nations had been living in the southeastern United States but were forced from their native lands by President Andrew Jackson.

One hundred thousand Native Americans had

to move west, to what was called "Indian Territory." Some Native Americans brought with them enslaved Black people who were freed after the Civil War ended. Many remained in Oklahoma.

Indian Territory in Oklahoma, 1855

Their children and their children's children often started their own towns. Between the end of the Civil War and 1920, more than fifty Black townships had sprung up. (Thirteen of these towns remain today.)

Ida E. Glenn

Ida E. Glenn, a citizen of the Creek Nation, with her husband, Robert, owned land just south of Tulsa. Their land turned out to be very special, because under it, there was oil. Lots of it. The sort of oil that could heat homes and run cars after it was refined.

In 1905, Ida and Robert were paid $45 (which would be almost $1,400 today) for a lease to their land. They also received part of the money made from the oil drilled on it. The surrounding land was named after them: Glenpool. It's a town that stands even today. This is only one example of the good fortune Black people in Oklahoma found.

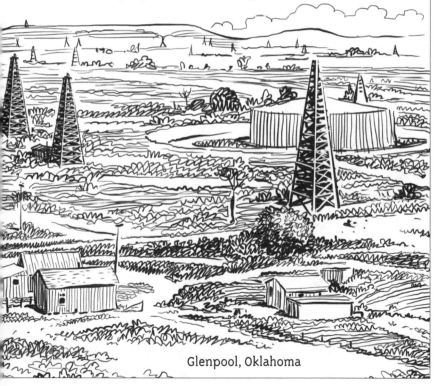

Glenpool, Oklahoma

From 1865 to 1877, the United States government carried out programs to help roughly four million newly freed people in the South, as well as in Indian Territory. This period of history is known as Reconstruction. But attempts to make life better for Black people were seen by many white people as unfair.

Black people were able to go to school
for the first time during the Reconstruction era.

White politicians and voters soon passed laws to make life as hard as possible for Black people. For example, certain laws made it essentially impossible for Black people in the South to vote or get good jobs.

Because of this, many Black people in the 1880s, 1890s, and early 1900s decided to leave the South behind. Many ended up relocating to Oklahoma and Kansas. In 1906, a wealthy Black landowner named O. W. Gurley bought forty acres of land in Tulsa and named the area Greenwood. He sold some of this land to other

O. W. Gurley

Black people, who built homes and businesses.

Oil was discovered in Oklahoma in the late 1890s. Oil still impacts our lives today. It fuels

our cars, heats our homes, and even creates the asphalt for paving our roads. Soon, Tulsa became known as the "Oil Capital of the World." People came to work in the oil fields. Those people also needed barbershops, grocery stores, restaurants, and more. Because of oil, the city of Tulsa grew rapidly. The city's population rose from 18,000 in 1910 to 140,000 by 1930.

The Exodusters

"Exodusters" was a name given to Black people who had lived primarily in Mississippi, Louisiana, Tennessee, and Texas before deciding to move west. Soon after the end of Reconstruction, they moved to Kansas, Oklahoma, and Colorado. There were as many as forty thousand Exodusters. Black communities were founded and grew in all of Oklahoma's larger cities. One of these communities was Greenwood, in the northern part of Tulsa.

Not only did Tulsa keep growing but Black Wall Street did, too. Black people created their own neighborhood because they were not allowed to own houses in white areas; they couldn't start their own businesses there. If their jobs were in white neighborhoods, they had to use bathrooms with signs that said, "For Coloreds."

By 1921, residents of Greenwood could watch a play at the Dixie Theatre or a movie at the Williams Dreamland Theatre. They could

go for sandwiches at Little Pullman Cafe or treat themselves to waffles at the local waffle house. The Stradford Hotel had fifty-four rooms and was considered one of the finest Black hotels in the country. On street after street, Black people were shopping at mainly Black-owned businesses. Down one street was Loula Williams's confectionery. (A confectionery is a store that sells candy and ice cream.) Down another was Rebecca Brown Crutcher's barbecue pit. It welcomed

home men working in the oil fields just miles out of the city. Within Greenwood, not every person was growing rich. But many were.

This sense of opportunity, within a mostly segregated country, appealed to many Black people long after the Exodusters had set their sights westward.

Just outside of Tulsa, another small Black community called Red Bird published brochures to get more people to come. The brochures described the great wonders of Black life in the small town. One read, "A Message to the Colored Man . . . Do you want a home in the Great Southwest—The Beautiful Indian Territory? In a town populated by intelligent, self-reliant colored people?" In the brochure, a minister named Jason Mayer Conner wrote of his own experience, "I have made a personal visit to the Indian Territory

and know it to be the best place on earth for the negro." Others said that "this country is the Paradise for the colored man." The words *Negro* and *colored* were commonly used in the 1900s, but they are considered offensive today.

Newspapers like the Black-owned *Muskogee Comet* reported that this part of Oklahoma "may verily be called the Eden of the West for the colored people." A newspaper in Kansas called the *Afro-American Advocate* pleaded with Black people far and wide to "come home, come home . . . Come out of the wilderness from among these lawless lynchers and breathe the free air."

In Greenwood, stories about people like

Mabel Little proved that these claims were true. Mabel's grandparents had been enslaved. She came to Tulsa with not much at all. It was rough at first—she could barely afford to rent a room in a boardinghouse. But Mabel got a job working at a hotel.

Mabel Little

Soon after, she met a man named Pressley, who shined shoes. They got married and saved up enough money to buy a small three-room house. Pressley ran his shoe-shining business in one room of the house. Mabel opened her own beauty shop in another. It had a staff of three and was later

featured in the famous Black magazine *Ebony*. The couple bought a Ford Model T car.

The Ford Model T

In 1921, owning a car was still a big deal. Only well-off families like the Sims and the Littles could afford one. It was Henry Ford who started using assembly lines to manufacture automobiles quickly and cheaply so that average Americans could hope to get behind the wheel of their own car. In 1924, the Ford Motor Company produced almost two million of their popular black Model T. It cost $295 (approximately $5,000 today).

Ford Model T car from the 1920s

By the time of the massacre, Mabel and her husband had made it: They had built a five-bedroom home. Her husband opened his own restaurant, and the couple rented out two other houses that they owned.

The only remaining 1920s home in Greenwood is now the Mabel B. Little Heritage House

Stories like these were not uncommon in Greenwood. But they all came to a bitter and sad end.

CHAPTER 2
Danger!

Yes, there was great opportunity on Black Wall Street. However, throughout the state of Oklahoma, laws treated Black people as second-class citizens. These laws existed all over the South as well.

The Oklahoma state government, run by white men, did not want integration. (Integration means people of all races living together as equals.)

After Oklahoma became a state in 1907, the very first bill that the state senate passed was called "the coach law."

"The coach law" required trains to provide separate cars (known as coaches) for white people and Black people. Right away, the new state was doing what it could to keep Black people apart from white people. (This is called segregation.) In addition, each railroad station and bus depot had to have separate waiting rooms.

Separate bathrooms, too. If this didn't happen, the railroad or bus company would have to pay a fine between $100 and $1,000. (In today's money that would equal $3,000 to $30,000.) And the fines didn't stop there. If a Black person was caught disobeying the law—for instance, using the white restroom at the railroad station—they could be fined, too, anywhere from $5 to $25. (That amounts to about $150 to $750.)

Does that sound like a lot? Does that seem fair? Think about it this way: In 2021, the average speeding ticket—the penalty for endangering people's lives—costs a driver about $150.

This was Oklahoma's first law and its first "Jim Crow law."

Jim Crow laws were laws that cities, counties, and states passed to keep Black people separated from white people. These laws took back the opportunities gained by Black people during Reconstruction. Because of Jim Crow laws,

Black patients couldn't go to hospitals for white people. They couldn't stay in the same hotels or be served at restaurants that had signs that said, "For Whites Only." They had to sit in the back of movie theaters and public buses. Perhaps worst of all, Black schoolkids couldn't attend schools for white students. Jim Crow laws weren't overturned until the 1950s and 1960s.

Who Was Jim Crow?

The laws separating Black people from white people were named after a character in song and dance shows of the 1800s. These shows were for white audiences. Jim Crow was always played by a white actor wearing black makeup on their face, which is known as blackface. He made fun of Black people by acting lazy and silly.

The coach law passed in the state senate of Oklahoma, thirty-seven to two. It lasted until 1965.

It wasn't just the coach law that made living in Tulsa dangerous for Black people. People should never be harassed for being who they are. The growth and prosperity of the Black community there angered some white people. It made them jealous. They wanted to take out their anger and jealousy by attacking well-off Black folks. This held true not only in Oklahoma, but in many other parts of the country as well.

Besides moving west, Black people also left the South to find better opportunities in big cities in the North, like Detroit, Chicago, and New York City. By the time World War I ended in 1918, five hundred thousand Black people were living in these cities. There, too, they faced prejudice and anger. Thousands of white soldiers returned home from the battlefields of Europe. They falsely assumed that though Black men had served in the military, Black people were taking jobs they thought belonged to them. They were angry about this. Very angry. Relations between the races worsened.

The tension was stoked further by members of hate groups, like the Ku Klux Klan, who believed in white supremacy. (This is the mistaken notion that white people are better than people of other races.)

Ku Klux Klan

The Ku Klux Klan is an American hate group that targets nearly every type of person who is not a white Christian man. It first formed after the Civil War, during Reconstruction, when Black people won their rights as citizens. Members of the KKK wore white robes and white hoods that covered

their faces. They burned homes and killed innocent Black people. The very first hit movie, which was released in 1915, portrayed the KKK as heroes. It was called *The Birth of a Nation*.

Though there are still chapters of the KKK around the country, other groups have now emerged with similar goals and aims, like the Patriot Front, the Proud Boys, and many others.

The Ku Klux Klan carried out sixty-four lynchings in 1918 and eighty-three in 1919. A lynching is when a mob—not a judge and jury in a courtroom—decides someone has committed a crime and kills them. Lynchings were barbaric, unlawful executions usually done by hanging victims from a tree. If police officers were on hand, they often participated, claiming they were carrying out justice.

Lynchings were meant to terrorize and control Black people in the nineteenth and twentieth centuries. Most lynchings took place in the South. The unspoken message was: "If you don't watch your step, this could happen to you." Although it seems hard to believe, lynchings were public events attended by crowds of white people—men, women, and young children. Some people would take photos of a lynching and put them onto postcards, which were then widely distributed as souvenirs.

The summer of 1919 became known as the "Red Summer" because of all the blood spilled in race riots. They broke out in such cities as Washington, DC; Omaha, Nebraska; and Knoxville, Tennessee. One of the worst and perhaps the most well-known took place in Chicago, Illinois. That city's Black population had

A Black man is questioned during Chicago race riot, 1919

increased from 44,000 in 1909 to over 100,000 in 1919. Anger had been building as competition for jobs in the city's stockyards (where meat was butchered and packaged) grew. Though moments of racial violence have many reasons for starting, this Chicago riot started with the stoning and drowning of a Black teenager. As Black people protested because such an awful thing happened, they were met with violence by a white mob. Like in Black Wall Street, white people sparked Black people to protest only to eventually launch a violent assault on Black people. In all, in Chicago, 38 people were left dead, including 23 Black men and boys, and 537 more were injured, of whom 342 were Black. A thousand more Black families were left homeless.

Two years later, in Greenwood, a seemingly unimportant incident lit a fire that engulfed Black Wall Street and destroyed it. In eighteen hours, it was gone.

CHAPTER 3
The Deadly Spark

For nineteen-year-old Dick Rowland, May 30, 1921, likely started out no different from any other day. He had a job shining shoes in the white part of Tulsa, just south of where he lived. Like Veneice, Dick had attended Booker T. Washington High School, where he'd been a football star. But Dick didn't take to school like some other kids. He dropped out and started working. Shining shoes paid him decent enough money. As hard as Dick worked, he felt the effects of

Dick Rowland

Oklahoma Senate Bill One—the coach law. He and his fellow workers had no choice but to use a bathroom outside of the shoeshine shop—one for Black people.

The Drexel Building in downtown Tulsa was not far from where he worked. A department store was on the bottom two floors. It was one of

Drexel Building

the few buildings that had a restroom for Black people. On that day in May, Dick very well could have wanted to use the restroom. But regardless of his reason, when he entered the elevator in the Drexel Building, his life would be forever changed.

The elevator was operated by a girl named Sarah Page. She was seventeen, not much younger than Dick. But Sarah was white.

Back then, elevators in tall buildings and big stores weren't automatic. People were hired to operate them. Often, they wore a uniform. Elevator operators had to manage the speed of the elevator and make sure that it would stop properly at each floor. And in some buildings, elevator operators like Sarah would often greet passengers. In department stores, they might announce special sales offered on different floors.

No one knows exactly what happened in the elevator. It's very possible that Dick tripped into

Sarah by accident. At some point Sarah screamed, a scream loud enough for a clerk at the department store to hear. Dick Rowland fled from the Drexel Building.

The clerk had not seen anything. Nevertheless, he reported the incident, saying that Dick Rowland assaulted Sarah Page. (An assault is an attack.) The next day, the *Tulsa Tribune,* a white newspaper, ran a racist headline on its front page. The newspaper had no way of knowing if anything had happened to Sarah Page. The headline in the *Tulsa Tribune* read, "Nab Negro for Attacking Girl in

an Elevator." The article went on to report that Dick had "attacked her, scratching her hands and face and tearing her clothes." None of this was true. In fact, later on, the newspaper editor even admitted that the article was made up. Sarah herself never accused Dick of a crime and later denied anything had happened in the elevator.

A lot of readers, however, believed the story. Back then, a local paper was the way most people learned the news. Also, some white people may have wanted the *Tulsa Tribune's* article to be true.

It would confirm all the worst things they believed young Black men would do.

The morning of May 31, Dick Rowland was arrested and taken downtown. He was booked at the police station and then transferred to the county courthouse, where he was put in a jail cell on the top floor.

A mob of white men had decided to take the law into their own hands.

CHAPTER 4
The Shot Heard 'Round Tulsa

By about six or seven p.m. on May 31, a group of about three hundred white Tulsans gathered at the courthouse. According to the Oklahoma Historical Society, the crowd wanted Dick Rowland handed over to them. Although the

sheriff told the crowd to leave, it didn't. Instead, it grew to about four hundred people.

Hearing what was going on, about twenty-five men from Greenwood drove over to the courthouse. They wanted to make sure that Dick Rowland was protected and would receive a fair trial. Most of these Greenwood men had been soldiers in World War I. Many were believed to be carrying firearms.

In an eyewitness account of the events, a man named William "Choc" Phillips wrote that he remembered the sheriff saying to this group of Black men, "I am the sheriff of Tulsa County. Now you men in the street listen to me. Go home before a lot of people get hurt. You have no business coming up here and parading around

William "Choc" Phillips

with these guns like this. If you are law-abiding people, you will go home before some real trouble starts."

After that, Choc remembers hearing one of the Black men saying, "We'll go home when we get that Negro boy [Dick Rowland] you all want to lynch." And another Black man echoed, saying, "That's right, and we ain't goin' nowhere

without him." Not one Black person believed Dick Rowland would get justice—there'd be no trial in a courtroom with a lawyer to defend him, and no jury to decide on a verdict.

The men of Greenwood had every reason to fear what a crowd of angry white men would do, because of a man named Roy Belton.

Roy Belton

Roy Belton had been a white prisoner in the Tulsa courthouse about a year before Dick Rowland was arrested and jailed there. Roy Belton had been convicted of killing another white man. A white mob stormed the courthouse, grabbed Roy Belton, and wasted no time lynching him. To people in Greenwood, this proved how much danger Dick Rowland was in. If a white man had been lynched, imagine what a mob would do to somebody Black.

Even so, the men of Greenwood—whose protest had been peaceful—turned back for home. Later that same night, however, word got to them that the white mob had grown much bigger and was trying to storm the courthouse. How big was the mob? Estimates of its size range

from one thousand to two thousand people. So, a group of Greenwood men—about seventy-five this time—returned to the courthouse. The Black men offered to help the sheriff keep peace, and again the sheriff told them to go home.

Again, the Black men turned to leave. But right

after that, the real trouble started. All at once, a white man confronted one of the Black veterans holding a pistol and tried to seize it. A shot was fired. Exactly how it happened is not known.

However, in no time, twelve people lay dead. And this was just the beginning. That one shot led to the deaths of three hundred Black Tulsans (that we know of), injured eight hundred more, and set off a blaze that left Greenwood no more than a mass of charred, broken bricks.

CHAPTER 5
The Invasion of Greenwood

After the shot was fired and a dozen men were struck dead, Greenwood became a battlefield. Over the next fourteen hours, homes were burned to the ground. There were reports of children hiding under their beds hoping to keep safe. There were people who ran to their basements while above them they could smell smoke from the fires destroying their homes. Women fled from their houses into the streets, still in their nightgowns. Churches were ransacked and stores were looted before being torched.

Lessie Benningfield Randle, who people in Tulsa now call "Mother Randle," was six years old when this massacre happened. In a 2021 interview with the news website *Andscape*, at 106 years old,

she recounted how the
white mob "ran us from
one place to the other,
chased us like hounds
chasing a rabbit." She
recalled, "I saw people
shoot people down on
the street. I saw people
running, I saw bodies, I
saw them kill the people

Lessie Benningfield Randle

and shoot people down. On one end of the street,
they just tied them up until somebody could
come pick them up in a truck. I was quite small

and I don't remember a whole lot, but I never want to see it again, I know that."

Where were the police? What were they doing to help the people of Greenwood? The answer is nothing. They joined the mob. Also, the police force quickly made hundreds of white men "deputies," giving them guns as well as badges. These deputies helped white rioters trying to take down every Black resident they could find. Many Black residents were killed trying to defend their homes, themselves, and their families.

Many in Greenwood saw small private planes buzzing low in the sky. One was almost certainly owned by the Sinclair Oil Company. The planes were keeping track of the movements of Black Tulsans, shooting at them as well as dropping bombs of turpentine that exploded on the ground, setting more fires.

Mary E. Jones Parrish

Mary E. Jones Parrish was a Black woman and a journalist. She collected eyewitness accounts of the Tulsa Race Massacre in her book, *Events of the Tulsa Disaster*. Mary remembered that there were planes "out of the sheds, all in readiness for flying, and these men with high-powered rifles were getting into them." The planes were shooting down on people. Another resident recalled that "more than a dozen aeroplanes went up and began to drop turpentine balls upon the Negro residences." Flying low, "they left the entire block a mass of flame."

EVENTS OF THE TULSA DISASTER

BY
MRS. MARY E. JONES PARRISH

By noon the next day, gone was Loula Williams's confectionery on North Greenwood Avenue. Gone were the Dreamland and Dixie theaters. The Little Pullman Cafe was now only a memory, as was the Stradford Hotel.

One thousand homes—and everything in them—were destroyed. The thirty-five square blocks of Black Wall Street were rubble, fires still smoldering everywhere. There were bodies of Black people lying in the streets. Veneice Sims was lucky: Her parents loaded up their car and took off.

Many in Greenwood stayed behind and tried to help the wounded and dying, offering what medical aid they could. They showed great

heroism. And though some departed, some returned, like Veneice Sims and her family, who came back to help the wounded.

A man known as Horace "Peg Leg" Taylor was among the residents fighting for their homes. Peg Leg was a Black war veteran. His real name was Horace Greeley Beecher Taylor and he survived the massacre. Exactly what he did during it remains the stuff of legend.

The story goes that, as the white mob made its way into Greenwood, Peg Leg started stealing weaponry from a general store nearby called Dick Barton's. It was white-owned and sold ammunition. The story goes that all through the day on Tuesday and on through Wednesday morning, Peg Leg managed to return to Dick Barton's again and again for more ammunition. Somehow, he pulled this off while the staff helped white rioters buy weapons. Peg Leg managed to steal enough ammunition—rounds and rounds

of it—for the Black defenders of Greenwood to hold off the mob.

Peg Leg, along with others, took control of the hill that was just blocks north from where the white mob was creating its plan to invade. From the high ground, Peg Leg and the other men on the hill made their stand against the murderous crowd down below.

The story goes that Peg Leg was left alone on the hill for six hours. Even so, he stood his ground and never stopped shooting. In fact, it is said that he got off so many rounds of bullets taken from Dick Barton's store that people thought he must be using a machine gun. Not pistols. The white invaders couldn't believe it was just one man fighting them. They felt sure that Peg Leg must have gotten reinforcements to help. Supposedly, the white rioters ended up begging for a ceasefire and even promised to let go of the Black people they had captured. Peg Leg got away free. And without him, who knows? Maybe even more Black Tulsans would have died.

Another hero whose incredible bravery is remembered today was Dr. A. C. Jackson. He sacrificed his life helping victims of the massacre. He lived in Greenwood and worked at the area hospital. He was famous for his work performing surgery. He invented surgical tools that are still being used today. The founders of one of

Dr. A. C. Jackson

the top hospitals in the world (the Mayo Clinic in Minnesota) called Dr. Jackson the "most able Negro surgeon in America."

For hours during the destruction of Black Wall Street, Dr. Jackson stayed at the hospital, doing whatever he could for victims. Near the end of the massacre, at about 8:00 a.m., he finally went home. That was where a group of white men found him. Dr. Jackson did not have a gun. He raised his hands in the air, pleading, "Here am I. I want to go with you." But his words didn't stop the white rioters. Seven men came forward, two shot him, and the doctor later died of his wounds.

Dr. A. C. Jackson was just one of hundreds who died in an invasion sparked by ignorance, fear, and jealousy. In the middle of the night, the governor of Oklahoma got word of the massacre. He sent in soldiers from the state's National Guard. But they didn't arrive until nine o'clock the next morning. It was too late by then to stop the killing. Black Wall Street, as people had known it, was gone.

CHAPTER 6
Nothing Left?

All told, as many as three hundred Black people died, and some ten thousand others were left with nothing. More than one thousand

homes, schools, and businesses were brought to the ground.

As for the victims, who were they?

Unfortunately, even today, we still don't know the names of so many of those killed. Many were labeled as "unidentified." Others were described by their belongings or the way they'd died: "Burned Man 1," "Burned Man 2," or "Man with a Hat."

It's likely that right after the massacre many victims were buried in mass graves, bodies heaped on top of other bodies. There was never a marker or a tombstone, no memorial service to honor their lives. Tulsa's government had no interest in remembering Black Wall Street—neither its prominence nor its massacre.

All this destruction happened in less than a day—$1.8 million or so in property loss. That would amount to $27 million in today's dollars.

Booker T. Washington High School was taken over by the American Red Cross. It became the headquarters for relief activities. Approximately two thousand refugees were housed there temporarily. With all health facilities suddenly gone, Booker T. Washington became a hospital and dental clinic.

The city put more than four thousand Black Tulsans in tents by the fairgrounds or had them stay in the city's convention hall. Groups were led with their hands up, as if they were criminals. Conditions were so bad, doctors were worried the refugees would get sick.

The land that Greenwood had been built on was prime real estate. It was to the advantage of white Tulsans in the city government to try to cover up what had happened and lay the blame on the residents of Greenwood. In fact, for a very long time, the terrible event was known as the "Tulsa Race Riot," meaning the Black population had started the massacre. Even more shocking is that not a single white person in the mob was sent to prison.

Newspapers around the United States carried articles about the burning of Greenwood.

However, right away white leaders of Tulsa tried to signal to the outside world that all was well. Alva Niles was a white Tulsan who headed the local chamber of commerce. (That is an organization that represents the interests of businesses and business leaders.) Niles said that "a movement is now being organized, not only for the succor, protection and alleviation of the sufferings of the Negroes but to formulate a plan of reparation in order that homes may be rebuilt and families as nearly as possible rehabilitated." He was trying to convince the outside world not to worry; the business community of Tulsa was figuring out how to help the very Black people they hurt. These were false promises.

In fact, Tulsa mayor T. D. Evans reacted to this massacre with almost a sense of relief. A nearly destroyed Greenwood made replacing the prosperous Black neighborhood with a train station that much easier. Remember, Tulsa was growing, and Black Wall Street sat just above the city's downtown. Another train station could now rise over what had once been a thriving community. The mayor also said, "It was good generalship [leadership] to

T. D. Evans

let the destruction come to that section where the trouble was hatched up." He was placing the blame on Black victims of the massacre! As he saw it, with Greenwood gone, the future of Tulsa looked even brighter. "Let the Negro settlement be placed farther to the north and east," because in T. D. Evans's mind, Greenwood was more "well suited for industrial purposes than for residences."

There were people and organizations from outside of Tulsa that wanted to send money and aid to help the survivors of Greenwood. The *Chicago Tribune,* for example, offered to donate $1,000. The city of Tulsa, however, blocked these efforts.

Why did they do that?

Because by accepting the aid, city officials would be admitting that something terrible had indeed happened in Tulsa. Also, by denying outside aid for Black people, the city officials could stick to their lie that a Black riot was to blame for the destruction. If that were the case, the residents of Greenwood—and not the city—should have to pay the costs of rebuilding.

CHAPTER 7
No Help

The efforts of Black people to get repaid for all they'd lost were not successful. Their cases were stalled or dismissed by the courts. Later in June of 1921, a grand jury made a report on what had happened. A grand jury is a group of people chosen to decide if a crime has been committed, and if so, who is to blame. What did the grand jury's report decide? It blamed "armed Negroes" for the destruction.

While thousands of Black people were sitting in internment camps, they were also temporarily barred from rebuilding their homes. Attorney

Buck Colbert (BC) Franklin

Buck Colbert (BC) Franklin—even though he was kept in an internment camp for several days—set up a tent and began working to defend the rights of massacre victims. The city of Tulsa's government passed a fire ordinance that would have prevented Greenwood residents from rebuilding their homes and their district. Franklin took the city of Tulsa and the mayor to court, and ultimately won the case in the state supreme court. This allowed people to reconstruct Greenwood—to start rebuilding their homes and their businesses. Without this, Black Wall Street would have been destroyed permanently.

But BC didn't stop there. He even tried to get insurance money for the owners of businesses and homes in Greenwood. Unfortunately, this didn't happen. Even today, the descendants of the massacre's victims continue to try to get a legal ruling in their favor. So far that has not happened. In 2005, the United States Supreme Court refused to hear their case.

Reparations: Righting a Wrong

Reparation means righting a wrong by helping those who have been treated unjustly. One way of helping is to give money to victims of injustice. The US government has done this in certain, limited cases.

Because the United States and Japan were enemies in World War II, the US government forced innocent Japanese Americans from their homes and placed them in internment camps. Nearly half a century later, each of these citizens received $20,000 for what had been done to them.

Black Americans are the only people who have not received financial reparations for acts of racial injustice. First and worst, this includes the enslavement of millions, which went on for well over two hundred years.

Japanese families living in internment camps, 1940s

You may be wondering, "Didn't the Black people in Tulsa have insurance to cover the damage to their homes and businesses?" Many did, but insurance companies refused to pay for losses from the massacre.

Why?

Insurance companies back then could claim that they didn't have to pay for damage due to a riot. Loula Williams had eight different insurance policies for her theater and confectionery. She spent a year and a half suing insurance companies. She was paid back some of the money she spent to buy the insurance policies . . . but received no money to rebuild her properties.

CHAPTER 8
Greenwood Rises Again

The desire and strength to rebuild meant that those remaining in Greenwood could not be held back. Homes were reconstructed. By 1922, a little over a year after the massacre, Loula Williams reopened her Dreamland Theatre. The family's confectionery was also back in business. The local paper announced offices available on the corner of Greenwood Avenue and Archer Street. Another massacre survivor, Juanita Alexander Lewis-Hopkins, recalled that "North Tulsa after the [massacre] was even more impressive than before."

In 1925, Greenwood hosted the annual conference of Booker T. Washington's National Negro Business League (now called the National Business League). By 1942, more than two hundred Black businesses called the Greenwood District home again. By the 1940s, because of all the reconstruction, Black people had even more opportunity, and on a larger scale.

National Business League

Booker T. Washington founded the National Negro Business League in 1900. The League's mission was "to promote the commercial and financial development of the Negro." Its members included successful Black business people. Its

purpose was to help other Black people in businesses. By 1915, the League had six hundred chapters in thirty-four states around the country. In 1966, the organization was relaunched and rebranded as the National Business League. The organization is still dedicated to the economic empowerment of Black businesses, communities, and people.

Keeping alive the memory of this terrible moment in American history became very difficult. As years went by, there were fewer and fewer people left who had lived through the horror and could help make others aware of it. White Tulsans made sure the massacre was not covered in history books or mentioned as part of Tulsa's past.

While growing up in Tulsa, even I, a Black kid, never heard what had happened in my own town. I knew nothing about the tremendous success of Greenwood. Also, despite the rebuilding of Black Wall Street, Black Tulsans were pushed farther north, away from the areas where they could most easily prosper. The rebuilt Black Wall Street was also wiped out.

CHAPTER 9
Urban Renewal . . . Really?

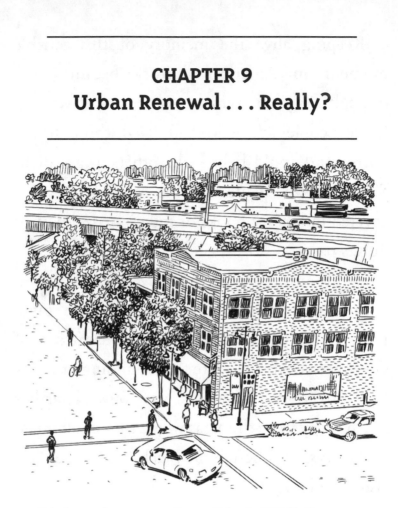

Today, the area where Black Wall Street once stood is considered one of the poorest, hardest-hit neighborhoods in Tulsa. Kids in this part of the city are likely to live almost eleven years less than kids in wealthier parts of Tulsa. The ability to get fresh food is limited and public transportation isn't within easy distance.

Again, how did this happen?

After half a century of growth, destruction, and restoration, the neighborhood of Greenwood was knocked down yet again. But this time it was not because of rioters, or fires, or any kind of violence. Instead, it happened because of public policy—decisions made by people in government who seemed not to care much about the lives of Black Tulsans.

From the 1950s through the early 1970s, *urban renewal* was the term for efforts to clear away slums and make way for affordable housing projects. Billions of dollars were spent to do this. It was happening all over the country. Whole neighborhoods were leveled. This meant urban renewal projects ended up displacing hundreds of thousands of people who had lived there.

Predominantly people of color in low-income neighborhoods. Urban renewal got the nickname "Negro Removal."

Through urban renewal, Black businesses, schools, and family homes in Tulsa were destroyed and replaced with two intersecting highways, I-244 and US-75. These highways created an easy way for white people in the suburbs surrounding the heart of Tulsa to drive into and out of the city. Eager developers and city leaders did not consider how much pain this would cause the Black people who had lived there previously. By 1979, in the Greenwood area, 76 percent of people who were forced to move were Black. Once again, Greenwood was never the same.

It's awfully hard for a person my age to imagine what Greenwood once looked like. It's the recollections of Tulsans that provide the best picture of what was taken away.

One Greenwood elder named Brenda Nails-Alford remembers a time when Black Wall Street was still the Black Wall Street she and so  many others knew. Her childhood home was replaced with a house from 1940, which came from a different part of Tulsa. In her words, "A little paint was thrown on it and that was called 'renewal.'"

Brenda Nails-Alford

CHAPTER 10
The Story Lives On

People like Brenda Nails-Alford refuse to let the story of Greenwood die. The traditions of storytelling and oral history in the Black community have kept up the calls for justice, even if justice was never served to the original residents or their descendants like Brenda.

As for Veneice Sims, whose happy childhood ended on May 31, 1921, she passed away with her family never having received any compensation for the pain inflicted on them on that awful day.

The Tulsa Race Massacre, however, is no longer kept a secret. It is a shameful incident that all Americans must deal with. Since the 1970s, the massacre started to be mentioned in school textbooks. Then, in 1997, Don Ross, a resident

Don Ross

of Greenwood and a then-member of the Oklahoma state legislature, pushed for a bill to study just what happened in 1921. Until then, many people still referred to the massacre as a "Negro uprising," if they even knew about it.

Before the late 1990s, very few eyewitness accounts from survivors of the massacre had been documented. No search had been approved to find those who were buried in mass graves. And no one had figured out exactly how much damage had been done and just how much people were owed.

Tulsa is as segregated today as it was in 1921. Don Ross has written, "Tulsa's race relations are more ceremonial—liken to a bad marriage, with spouses living in the same quarters but housed in different rooms, each escaping one another by perpetuating a separateness of silence." What Don Ross meant was that Tulsans may live together. They may even work together. But people still can't talk honestly about what bad things happened there. Nobody even talks about the amazing achievements people in Black Wall Street accomplished, both before and after the massacre. The report put together by Don Ross and his colleagues recommended "direct payments to riot survivors and descendants." That has never happened, though the push for compensation has only grown.

In 2011, community leaders and the city government opened the John Hope Franklin Reconciliation Park, named after the son of BC Franklin. John grew up in Tulsa and went on to

John Hope Franklin

become one of the nation's most well-known historians. In the early 1980s, he and one of his students, Scott Ellsworth, helped uncover many details about the massacre that hadn't been known before. That is why the Reconciliation Park was built in his honor. It is also to remember

TOWER
OF
RECONCILIATION
'Oklahoma - 1541 to the Present"

Sculpture by Ed Dwight

John Hope Franklin Reconciliation Park in Tulsa

the victims of the 1921 massacre. (*Reconciliation* means efforts to bring people back together.) At the center of the park is a twenty-six-foot-tall bronze structure. It's called the "Tower of Reconciliation" and honors the long history of Black people in Oklahoma.

In 2021, a hundred years after the massacre, and after years of raising tens of millions of dollars, a history center in Greenwood was opened. It's called "Greenwood Rising." However,

Greenwood Rising history center

many Black residents of Tulsa do not think that a park and a history center, no matter how beautiful, are enough to make up for what happened to the people of Black Wall Street.

Most Oklahoma schools still don't teach about the massacre. Not until a few years ago did the city of Tulsa begin efforts to search for the mass graves of victims.

As of 2023, Viola Fletcher was one of only three known residents of the original Greenwood still living. She was 107 years old when she was invited to speak to the US Congress in 2021. It was to talk about her pursuit for justice and compensation. Viola Fletcher thinks of it as reparations. "We live this history, and we can't ignore it," Viola said. She told Congress about what was lost because of the massacre: "I lost my chance of an education. I never finished school past the fourth grade. I have never made much money."

Viola Fletcher, who people in Tulsa call "Mother Fletcher," wasn't the only one to testify. Her younger brother, Hughes Van Ellis, also made plain the goal of the survivors and their descendants, people who were victims of the Tulsa Race Massacre. "You're taught that when something is stolen from you, you can go to the courts to be made whole," Hughes told the United States representatives. The hope has been to be compensated for their losses.

But that had been denied to Black Tulsans. Instead, they were made to feel they were unworthy of justice. With tears in his eyes, he said what so many Black people have felt for so long, whether in Tulsa or not: "We're not asking for a handout. We're asking for a chance to be treated like a first-class citizen."

Timeline of the Tulsa Race Massacre

1879 — Exodusters begin moving out of the southern United States and head out west

1906 — Greenwood neighborhood, also known as Black Wall Street, is founded

1907 — Oklahoma becomes a state

1920 — Lynching of white prisoner taken from Tulsa courthouse

1921 — May 30—A white store clerk claims Dick Rowland assaulted Sarah Page

— May 31—Dick Rowland is arrested

— Tulsa Race Massacre begins

— June 1—Tulsa Race Massacre concludes

— June 25—Oklahoma grand jury report blames Greenwood residents for the destruction

1922 — Rebuilding in Greenwood is well underway

1960s — Urban renewal begins in Tulsa and causes the destruction of many Black communities, including Greenwood

1997 — State legislator Don Ross pushes a bill to study the Tulsa Race Massacre

2021 — Viola Fletcher, a former resident of Greenwood, speaks to US Congress about reparations for Tulsa Race Massacre survivors, victims, and their families

Timeline of the World

1865– 1877	The Reconstruction era, in which the civil rights and constitutional rights of freedmen are addressed by the government after the Civil War
1884	Mark Twain publishes *The Adventures of Huckleberry Finn*
1906	Jazz Age dancer and singer Josephine Baker is born
1921	*The Kid*, starring Charlie Chaplin, is released in movie theaters
	Bessie Coleman becomes the first Black woman and first Native American woman to earn a pilot license
1922	Pharaoh Tutankhamun's tomb is found in Egypt
1942	President Joe Biden is born in Pennsylvania
1954	The Supreme Court strikes down segregation in the *Brown v. Board of Education* case
1955	The Vietnam War begins
1963	The March on Washington takes place, with Martin Luther King Jr. delivering his "I Have a Dream" speech
1997	Diana, Princess of Wales, is killed in a car crash in Paris
2009	Barack Obama becomes first Black president of the United States and serves until January 20, 2017
2021	The COVID-19 vaccine is given to billions of people worldwide

Bibliography

*Books for young readers

*Boston Weatherford, Carole. *Unspeakable: The Tulsa Race Massacre*. Minneapolis: Lerner Publishing Group, 2021.

Coates, Ta-Nehisi. "The Case for Reparations." *The Atlantic*, June 2014.

*Colbert, Brandy. *Black Birds in the Sky: The Story and Legacy of the 1921 Tulsa Race Massacre*. New York: Balzer + Bray, 2021.

Ellsworth, Scott. *Death in a Promised Land: The Tulsa Race Riot of 1921*. Baton Rouge, LA: LSU Press, 1982.

Ellsworth, Scott. *The Ground Breaking: An American City and Its Search for Justice*. New York: Dutton, 2021.

Gayle, Caleb. "100 Years After the Tulsa Massacre, What Does Justice Look Like?" *New York Times Magazine*, May 25, 2021. https://www.nytimes.com/2021/05/25/magazine/tulsa-race-massacre-1921-greenwood.html.

Gayle, Caleb. "The Neighborhood Fighting Not to Be Forgotten." *The Atlantic*, May 12, 2021. https://www.theatlantic.com/politics/archive/2021/05/fight-preserve-greenwood/618770/.

Gerkin, Steve. "Beno Hall: Tulsa's Den of Terror." *This Land*,
September 3, 2011. https://thislandpress.com/2011/09/03/
beno-hall-tulsas-den-of-terror/.

Hirsch, James S. *Riot and Remembrance: The Tulsa Race War
and Its Legacy*. New York: Houghton Mifflin Harcourt,
2002.

Johnson, Hannibal B. *Black Wall Street: From Riot to
Renaissance in Tulsa's Historic Greenwood District*.
Austin, TX: Eakin Press, 2007.

Jones Parrish, Mary E. *Events of the Tulsa Disaster*. Privately
printed, 1922.

O'Dell, Larry. "Senate Bill One," Oklahoma Historical Society.
https://www.okhistory.org/publications/enc/entry.
php?entry=SE017.

Oklahoma Commission to Study the Tulsa Race Riot of 1921.
*Tulsa Race Riot: A Report by the Oklahoma Commission
to Study the Tulsa Race Riot of 1921*. February 21, 2001.
https://www.okhistory.org/research/forms/freport.pdf.

Loula Williams (right)—owner of the Williams Confectionery—
and her family, 1910s

Williams Dreamland Theatre in Tulsa, Oklahoma,
before it was destroyed in the massacre

Oil field in Tulsa, Oklahoma, around 1915

Part of Greenwood District after the Tulsa Race Massacre, 1921

Church on fire during the massacre, 1921

American Red Cross hospital used after the massacre, 1921

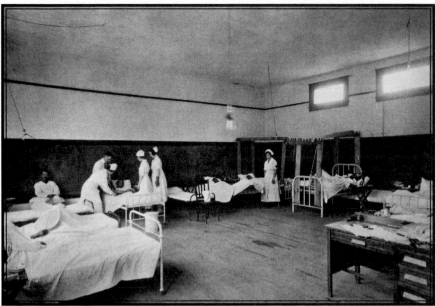

Surgical area of the Red Cross hospital after the massacre in Tulsa, 1921

Black woman is detained during the Tulsa massacre, 1921

Refugee camp in Tulsa, Oklahoma, after the massacre, 1921

People searching through rubble after the Tulsa Race Massacre, 1921

Newspaper headline about the massacre in Tulsa, printed on June 10, 1921

Greenwood Avenue rebuilt after the 1921 massacre

Williams Dreamland Theatre in Tulsa, Oklahoma, after it was rebuilt, 1930s

Grocery store and market in Tulsa, Oklahoma, that was rebuilt
after the massacre

Veneice Dunn Sims, a survivor of the 1921 Tulsa Race Massacre, 1999

Oklahoma State Representative Don Ross, 1999

Greenwood District of Tulsa, Oklahoma, 2020

MR. HUGHES VAN ELLIS

MS. VIOLA FLETCHER

Hughes Van Ellis (left) and Viola Fletcher (second right), survivors of the
Tulsa Race Massacre, testify before Congress, 2021.

Visitors view the Black Wall Street Memorial on Greenwood Avenue during the Tulsa Juneteenth Festival, 2021.